Meditations With NICHOLAS OF CUSA

Meditations With™

NICHOLAS of CUSA

translated
and adapted by
James Francis Yockey

Bear & Company
Santa Fe, New Mexico

To Mary, my soul-mate

Library of Congress Cataloging-in-Publication Data

Yockey, James Francis, 1962-
     Meditations with Nicholas of Cusa.

     1. Meditations. 2. Nicholas of Cusa, Cardinal, 1401-1464. I.
Nicholas, of Cusa, Cardinal, 1401-1464.
II. Title.
BX2182.2.Y57   1987   242   87-1256
ISBN 0-939680-40-8

Bear & Company, Inc.
PO Drawer 2860
Santa Fe, NM 87504

Design: Kathleen Katz
Illustrations: Jean and Richard Erdoes
Typography: Casa Sin Nombre, Santa Fe
Printed in the United States of America

CONTENTS

Publisher's Note:

Bear & Company is publishing this series of creation-centered mystic/prophets to bring to the attention and prayer of peoples today the power and energy of the holistic mystics of the western tradition. One reason western culture succumbs to boredom and to violence is that we are not being challenged by our religious traditions to be all we can be. This is also the reason that many sincere spiritual seekers go East for their mysticism—because the West is itself out of touch with its deepest spiritual guides. The format Bear & Company has chosen in which to present these holistic mystic/prophets is deliberate: We do not feel that more academically-styled books on our mystics is what everyday believers need. Rather, we wish to get our mystics of personal and social transformation off our dusty shelves and into the hearts and minds and bodies of our people. To do this we choose a format that is ideal for meditation, for imaging, for sharing in groups and in prayer occasions. We rely on primary sources for the texts but we let the author's words and images flow from her or his inner structure to our deep inner selves.

FOREWORD

When I reflect on a planet with 50,000 nuclear warheads, a planet where every continent is engaged in a deep and massive assault on the ecosystems, I have no doubt that our only way out of this pathology is to reinvent the human. Anything less is applying bandages to someone suffering from tuberculosis. We need fresh visions of who and what we are. We need insights that penetrate so deeply they show us how to leave behind the dead husks of consumerism, patriarchy, militarism, anthropocentrism, and materialism. Where can we go for assistance in our work of re-inventing ourselves?

Nicholas of Cusa offers us a cosmological vision that is fascinating, that promises to heal, that is both ancient and contemporary. I am speaking of his great vision of the universe as an *explicatio-complicatio* dynamism. As James Yockey translates:

> "Divinity is the enfolding
> of the universe, and the universe
> is the unfolding of divinity."

We, in the last part of the twentieth century, have an added advantage in our efforts to assimilate Nicholas's wisdom, for we have learned that the universe is in fact very much as he describes here. At least this is the understanding of some of the most impressive physicists of our time, notably David Bohm of Birbeck College, London, who cites Nicholas of Cusa as a precursor for his own work.

To appreciate this advance in understanding physical reality, one needs to recognize that the picture of an elementary particle as a billiard ball no longer makes sense of our experiences, now that we have entered the quantum realm. Particles are not autonomous and separate things localized in space and time, nor are particles continuously enduring objects. What is required is an entirely different way of thinking about elementary matter.

How can we picture particles? Particles are events that flash forth in space and time. For Bohm and others, quantum reality is best discussed with the notions of an implicate and an explicate order to the universe. The particles, the houses, the trees, the people about us exist in the explicate realm of the universe. But these structures have unfolded from an invisible, atemporal implicate realm. A proton is a momentary unfolding from the implicate order into the visible finite structure we call the proton; but after a brief existence, the explicate proton disappears back into the implicate order.

A proton, then, is both the explicate version that is manifest in the world, as well as a cloud of potential forms hovering in the implicate world, offering themselves as possibilities for the next embodiment. In each moment a new version of the proton unfolds. Since this new proton has a different quantum state, we speak of the proton's "quantum leap." It would be more accurate to speak of the proton's "new form," for the proton has not "leaped" from one place to another place; the proton rather is freshly emerged from the implicate world.

The cosmology of Nicholas of Cusa captures in some essential ways these most recent insights of contemporary physicists. But Nicholas goes beyond contemporary scientists when he speaks of the spirituality appropriate to this vision of the universe. And this is absolutely crucial. Knowledge of the universe is essential; but we need to complete our journey by living a life that celebrates the magnificence of the universe. As I taste this marvelous cascade of poetry that James Yockey brings to us, I am struck by the following three implications for life today.

With regard to our place on Earth, Nicholas writes:

> ". . .when in perceiving the sensible
> I realize that it is born from deeper realms"

There is the proper relationship of the human to the Earth. The rock, the sky, the sycamore—each sensible thing has been born from something deeper. Not just from an "implicate realm" but from the divine heart of reality, the supreme mystery of all. And if our relationship with the forest does not celebrate the origin of the forest, we are not yet truly alive to what is there before us. And what is before us? The primary revelation of God, the sacred explication of ultimate mystery.

What would the world be like if humans lived within the wisdom Nicholas celebrates? Could our one-dimensional consumerism continue? Could our assault on the Earth's beauty continue?

With regard to the nature of human work, Nicholas writes:

> ". . .the human mind
> is the all
> of its dreams."

In the *explicatio-complicatio* cosmology, the nature of God is revealed by creation since creation continually unfolds from God. In a similar way, our own human nature is revealed by our dreams and imaginations and creativity. We create who we are by the dreams we choose to guide our work in the world. A person is never just "doing a job;" a person's actions are always a revelation of soul. That is, there is no dualism between a person's "soul" and a person's creativity.

Imagine the sort of world we would live in if humans entered this wisdom of Nicholas; if we recognized once and for all that in our work we are not just "doing something," we are in truth announcing: "This is what I am!"

Finally, **with regard to education**, I would like to quote Nicholas's line:

> The universe is the creature."

And in fact, ". . . in any creature, all creatures are found." And there Nicholas sums up the essence of three centuries of modern scientific investigation of the universe. For we know now by empirical and rational investigation that in each human there are elements of the stars, there are the creative activities of the first organisms on Earth, there are the structures and inventions of the Cambrian explosion in complexity. To examine the nature and structure of a child's hand is to examine all twenty-billion years of cosmic creativity, back to the fireball explosion at the beginning of things.

Can we imagine a world where young humans, sitting in a parent's lap, learn that they are the universe brought into a special form? That they are intimately related to everything in the heavens and on Earth? Can we imagine a world where education at the primary level means introducing children to this stupendous truth Nicholas celebrates? So that they come to feel the embrace of the great community of being in which they participate, even as they draw each breath?

Such were my own responses. Many more await you as you enter the magic of Nicholas's vision. May your adventure bring you and all of us more deeply into the enchanted wisdom at the heart of the universe.

BRIAN SWIMME
INSTITUTE IN CULTURE AND CREATION SPIRITUALITY
HOLY NAMES COLLEGE, OAKLAND

"What do the living seek but life?
The existent but existence?
What does love seek but to be loved?"

INTRODUCTION

These lines scribed by Nicholas of Cusa, one of the greatest of the Rheno-Flemish mystics, poetically evoke the depth of the spiritual tradition which was his matrix. This spiritual tradition is rightly named "creation-centered spirituality" for it holds the quest for life, existence, and love as central to the creation of ourselves and the creation of the universe.

Yet, these words were written within and for a culture much like our own. Europe, in the late Middle Ages (like the United States in the 20th century), was caught up in immense upheaval. It was a culture whose life-support systems had been extremely degraded, whose political-economic system was in an advanced state of decay, and whose spirituality was permeated with necrophilia, the love of death.

In such a death-loving culture, anyone seeking life, existence, and love would be thrust into opposition with the status quo. Indeed, such a person would be considered subversive. Nevertheless, Nicholas of Cusa penned these words and lived his life not on the outside of European culture, but as a cardinal in the Roman Church (and as a papal legate at that!), embroiled in the most significant, religious, political, and cultural events of his time. Ironically, it is precisely because of his exalted position that his countercultural writings in creation-centered spirituality have survived. Because of the similarity between his time and ours, because of his privileged position in a time of turmoil, and because of the spiritual tradition he represents so well, Nicholas has much wisdom to teach us.

ABOUT CUSA

Nicholas was born some time between August of 1400 and 1401, and he died in August of 1464. Although not much is known of his early years, we do know that during much of his life he sought to synthesize diverse strains of thought in the spheres of politics, religion, science, and philosophy. In these spheres, he was utterly successful.

Nicholas began and advanced his career as a canon lawyer. In this capacity he made contact with a number of high-placed officials from Rome who were impressed with his scholarship and brilliance. But this alone would not have guaranteed his advancement into the corrupt halls of power in his time. Nicholas also had developed a reputation for finding and collecting ancient manuscripts. His avocation intrigued the papal humanists of Italy, who were in the process of recovering the classical texts of the West. Of humble origins, with no inherited social rank, Nicholas cunningly traded some manuscripts for advancement and financial security. His position secure, Nicholas tirelessly worked for reform and unity among the various factions in a church that was fast falling apart.

As a papal legate, his travels brought him in contact with many other religious traditions. From these contacts, Nicholas acquired a deep appreciation of the diverse cultures of the known world. This unusual sense of pluralism became a powerful force in Nicholas' writings and set him apart from many of his contemporaries.

In his intellectual and spiritual development, Nicholas was principally influenced by four major figures. Plato and Raymond Lull were his intellectual guides; his spiritual guides were Meister Eckhart and Hildegard of Bingen. Nicholas, however, did not experience a dichotomy between the rational and mystical. Rather, it was through an organic blending of mathematics, mysticism, and philosophy that his work acquired its power and originality.

Nicholas was introduced to Plato through the recovery of Platonic manuscripts. As more of the original texts were unearthed, a fuller picture and appreciation of Plato began to emerge. The revival of classical culture gifted Nicholas with a profound sense of historicity and his grasp of Platonic and Pythagorean philosophy was probably unequaled by anyone in his time.

Regarding Raymond Lull's influence, Nicholas owned more works and manuscripts of Lull's than of any other author. In fact, he acquired over one-fourth of all Lull's titles. Cusa appropriated Lull's mathematical and scientific insights and made them his own through theological adaptation. It is often difficult, therefore to determine where Lull's thought ends and Cusa's begins.[1]

Nicholas's own mysticism emerged out of the creation-centered tradition. His writings arepermeated with the spiritual themes of the Rhineland mystics whose influence on him has been constantly overlooked.[2] He was connected to this tradition in several ways.

First, Nicholas was born in the Rhineland. Cues, from which Cusa derives, is on the Mosselle River. As with Hildegard and Eckhart, Nicholas' upbringing in this lush environment imparted to him a profound understanding of the processes of nature.[3] Second, over the years Nicholas accumulated one of the largest private libraries in Europe, which included many manuscripts of Eckhart and Hildegard—texts heavily annotated in Nicholas' own handwriting. Third, there is increasing evidence that Nicholas was influenced by the radical third-order movements of the Middle Ages. For example, Nicholas' contemporary, Johannes Wenck, attacked Cusa for pantheism and heresy, explicitly linking Nicholas to the Beghards and Beguines.[4]

Finally, while much has been written concerning *De Docta Ignorantia* (On Learned Ignorance), in which Cusa brilliantly evokes God's ineffability, very little has been written on *De Coniecturis* (On The Conjectural Art), which was written nearly simultaneously with the *De Docta Ignorantia*.[5] *De Coniecturis* celebrates humanity's divine origin and likeness—a likeness only activated in the world of the earthly senses. Unfortunately, as with all mysticism in the western tradition, Nicholas has been translated and interpreted within the narrow hermeneutic of Fall/Redemption. This Fall/Redemption mentality denies the Earth, emphasizing divine transcendence to the exclusion of divine immanence. With the recovery of the creation-centered tradition, we now have a more balanced hermeneutic in which to interpret the great mystics of the West. In this context, let us explore some of Nicholas's central conceptions.

ABOUT MIND AND THE UNIVERSE

At the center of Cusa's mysticism is the activity of mind. By "mind," Nicholas means much more than the ratiocinative faculty. Mind is a comprehensive term denoting the multidimensional modes of human and divine creative activity.[6]

According to Cusa, in order for mind to know anything, it must "liken" (*assimilare*) things to itself.[7] However, "To make like" is an inadequate translation of "assimilare." For Nicholas comes from the creation-centered tradition which has its roots in the wisdom literature of the Hebrew Scriptures, which, in turn, has its roots in prepatriarchal cultures.[8] In this heritage, knowing is best understood as tasting. For example, in Psalms, we read "taste and see the goodness of the Lord." The only way to know God in this tradition is to taste God. In fact, the words for "wisdom" in Latin (*sapientia*) and Hebrew (*Hokmah*) come from the verb to taste. *Assimilare* is better translated "to digest." Nicholas writes:

The mind digests things in the same way it assimilates visible things in seeing, audible things in hearing, flavorful things in tasting, odorous things in smell, touchable things in touch, sensible things in sense, imaginable things in imagination, and reasonable things in reason.[9]

So mind is not a passive principle waiting to be fed. Rather, mind is a "natural appetite" seeking out physical, cultural, and spiritual food.[10] While Nicholas affirms the desire to taste and therefore to know at all levels of human activity, he also recognizes that the most delicious cuisine on the menu is the spiritual one—divinity. Our greatest appetite is for God.

In attempting to ingest divinity, mind becomes the dynamic and formative principle within us (*anima*) which is expressed as creative, living activity outside of us (*animal*).[11] Thus the products of our creative activities are living entities, not merely things! Mind is the soul—the animating energy—which is both within and without. For Nicholas, as for Eckhart, the soul is less in the body than the body is in the soul.

Mind is panentheistic.[12] Cusa says: "Mind itself supposing itself to encompass, survey, and comprehend all things thus concludes that it is in everything and everything is in it."[13]

In sum, Nicholas asserts that we are panentheistically animated beings who, through the multidimensional digestion of divinity, i.e., creative activity, animate other beings. But what is the significance of such activity? Nicholas explains:

When indeed the human mind, the high likeness of God, participates as it is able in the fertility of the creative nature, it puts forth from itself, as the image of the all-powerful form, symbolic entities in the likeness of real beings. Thus, the human mind is the form of the symbolic world, just as the divine mind is that of the real world.[14]

When we creatively participate in the world, we enter into our divinity. We are *mens imago* Dei, "mind in the image of the divine." Yet, divinity still remains undigested. How can this be?

In a paradoxical twist, Nicholas says that while human creative activity participates in truth or God, it is not truth itself. God is, finally, indigestible. It is as if we could only smell the delectable aroma of our favorite food without fully tasting it. This is our plight—to have a ravenous appetite for divinity and yet never to taste divinity fully.

God, however, does not simply leave us frustrated. For the activity of the mind is not simply an anthropocentric dynamic. The dynamics of the mind drive the cosmos—the Earth and the heavens. The entire created order is caught up in the Cosmic Mind.

The characteristics of this dynamic are explained by Nicholas as a dynamic of flux: The universe is in constant motion or fluctuation. He uses the terms *complicatio* (enfolding) and *explicatio* (unfolding) to explain the flux. God is the enfolding (*complicatio*) of all created reality, and all created reality is the unfolding (*explicatio*) of God.[15] Humanity is the intersection of this interconnected macrocosm/microcosm. Yet, Nicholas's language suggests an even deeper relationship. For example, *complicare* means "to fold." This term in the Middle Ages was often used to describe the folding of hands. The image suggested is one of: the Divine hands folded around the cosmos. Additionally, *complicatio* has the further meanings of intricacy and confusion, from which is derived the English word, complication. So creation within the intimacy of God's hands is no simple task; indeed, it is very intricate and complicated and even confusing! The beautiful complementary images of God as artist and mother are evoked in a single word.

As to God's unfolding, Nicholas is no less eloquent. *Explicare* means "to unfold" or "uncoil." Both words speak to the constant creativity in the cosmic unfurling. They speak of creation happening not just once, but as the endless unfolding of God's treasures, or the uncoiling of a luxuriant carpet of unimaginable diversity rolling out into infinity. Important, too, is the notion of *explicatio* as explication or explanation. The created order explicates God. God is explained in the unfolding of the universe! It follows, therefore, that each creature is needed to explain the whole. Nicholas echoes Eckhart that "every creature is a word of God."[16]

In revealing the dynamics of the Cosmic Mind, Nicholas moves humanity beyond the frustration of never tasting God. Cusa states: "You created along with humanity all those things through which we, aroused by the things which delight our senses, are able to raise the eyes of our minds to you."[17] Thus, "The human mind is the enfolding of its dream world and its dream world is the unfolding of the human mind."[18]

Nicholas concludes that when humans enter fully into creative imagination (the divine digestive process) and activate this imagination in the world of the senses, we reach a threshold of truth. As we digest divine energies, authentically activating our creative capacities over time, we begin to take on the essences of that which we create (digest). When this happens, a deeper dimension of mind develops. Nicholas calls this deeper dimension "mind in simplicity" or Wisdom.[19] Mind in simplicity is potentially all things, but it does not operate to digest things; rather, it digests itself so that it may be assimilated into each thing. Nicholas explains:

Up to this point mind is not sated by this way of knowing [i.e., digesting] for it has no ultimate grasp of the exact truth of everything. . . Mind sees that this way of being is not truth itself but a participation in truth. Mind looks to its own simplicity. . .Then it employs this simplicity as an instrument so that it may digest itself to everything. . .In this fashion, mind grasps everything intuitively in its own simplicity.[20]

Therefore, wisdom is entered into when we move from actively digesting to being digested—from eating to being eaten—from creating to being created. And so Cusa states: "In this way it [mind] grasps intuitively everything as one, and itself as the assimilation of that One which is all."[21]

For those willing to make the spiritual journey along with him, Nicholas simply says. . . *Bon Apetit!*

ABOUT THE STRUCTURE

The structure of this book derives from the fourfold path

DIAGRAM A

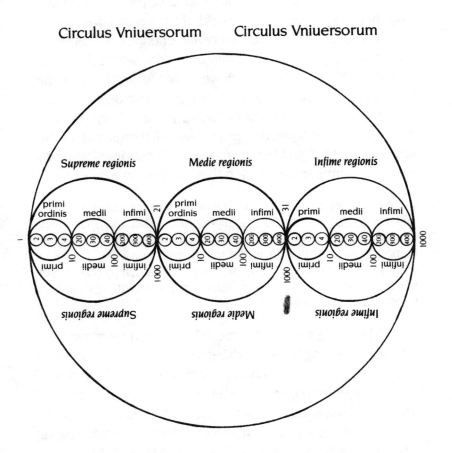

recovered by Matthew Fox in his translation of Meister Eckhart.[22] I say recovered instead of discovered because the fourfold path is explicit in Nicholas's mysticism, making it at least 500 years old. Nicholas states that, "Mind unfolds in a fourfold progression of natural flux."[23] In this diagram, Nicholas illustrates the spirals from which we move into ever-deeper wisdom. (Diagram A) What is perhaps most intriguing in this pattern is that cosmologists today are beginning to see the same fourfold pattern of natural flux in the unfolding of the universe, i.e., 1,2,3,4/1,2,3,4/1.[24]

These meditations follow the unfolding of mind through the four paths. Once through the four paths, we spiral back to revisit the first path. The paths of this journey are:

1. The Via Positiva
2. The Via Negativa
3. The Via Creativa
4. The Via Transformativa
1. The Via Speculativa

The Via Positiva In this path, Nicholas celebrates mind in the image of God/dess. Humanmindedness is the fruit of the Earth, which reflects the Divine Mind upon whose wisdom we are forever nurtured.

The Via Negativa In this path, we discover not the "learned ignorance" of scholarly detachment, but the "mindful ignorance" of facing (as Eckhart describes it) "a superessential darkness." No matter how connected we are to divinity, God is radically ineffable and unknowable.

The Via Creativa Through the mind of the lay street artisan, Nicholas urges us to trust God's ineffability by moving us into the depths of the creative process. In this process wisdom will be found.

The Via Transformativa In entering into the creative process, we connect with cosmic dynamics and more specifically with the dynamics of the Earth. Organic unity within rich diversity is the key to the transformation of personal/social reality. The immense difference between creation-centered spirituality and sentimental western piety is evoked by Nicholas in this path. Whereas, retreatist, sentimental mysticism claims that "peace is living in contemplation," Nicholas asserts that, "contemplation is living in peace." This is Earth-Mind.

The Via Speculativa The word *speculum* means mirror.[25] Prepatriarchal mythology and symbology used the or looking glass as a central symbol of creativity. For example, in the Middle Eastern creation myth concerning the Goddess Ashteroth or Tamar, it is said that the universe was created when she gazed upon herself in a mirror. Furthermore, in pre-Yahweh Hebrew myth, the Goddess Shekinah (the cosmic energy) created the Goddess Kether (omnipotent light), who then created a sister Chokmah (Wisdom). By looking into the eyes of her sister Chokmah, Kether created the universe.

The emergence of patriarchy reversed the life-giving symbol of the mirror into a symbol of superficial vanity and death. Thus we read of Medusa, whose visage turns those who see her to stone and who is killed by seeing her reflection in Perseus' mirror. There is also the fate of Narcissus, and the witch-burning Church Fathers' decree that the mirror is the devil's instrument.[26]

Despite those reversals of meaning, the mirror has deep and positive meaning for Cusa. The mirror is essentially a twofold symbol of critical consciousness on the one hand, and the "image of God/dess theme" on the other.

After moving through the four paths, we again enter into the image of God. We are the mirror-image of this paradigm. Once through these four paths, our self-consciousness is raised as the reflection of the divine image spread out through the cosmos. Thus we embark on the path of self-reflection. We become conscious of ourselves as the created order reflected back upon ourselves. Therefore, the universe, through us, becomes conscious of itself.

ABOUT GOD LANGUAGE

It has become clear from my reading of Nicholas that his religious language is loaded with the language of Wisdom (*sapientia*). Nicholas's God is a Sophia God—a Wisdom divinity. This wisdom tradition (unlike the habitual sexism of patriarchal scholarship) not only includes the "feminine" dimension of the Divine, but explicitly celebrates femaleness *as the Divine*. While Hildegard was deeper in this tradition than Nicholas, he is, nevertheless, unmistakably rooted in it as well. Because of this, I use the word "God/dess" to explicitly name and affirm the fact of female divinity.

ABOUT THE TEXT

All of this text except for the sermons, was translated from the Latin of Paul Wilpert, ed., Nikolaus von Kues Werke, Vols. I and II (Berlin: Walter De Gruyter & Co., 1967) which contains the Strassburg edition of 1488. This has been cross-referenced with the Heidelberg critical edition of Nicholas's collected works. Passages from Nicholas's sermons were taken from James Biechler, *The Religious Language of Nicholas of Cusa* (1975). The appendix at the end of this book indicates title, book (where applicable), chapter (where applicable), and page numbers as they appear in Wilpert for each of my translations. Additionally, I must acknowledge an indebtedness to Emma Salter's rendering of De Visione Dei, which, however outdated, is one of the few translations of Cusa that attempts to create a poetic or meditative atmosphere.

The arrangements and adaptions of Nicholas's words are my own. Like all the Meditations With, I make no apologies for my interpretive paraphrasing of this great mystic. Nicholas perhaps says it best: "It is necessary for one who wants to attain understanding to raise the intellect above the meaning of words. . .which in any case cannot be properly adapted to such great mindful mysteries." Amen!

NOTES

[1]For a discussion of this problem of influence, see I. N. Hilgarth, *Ramon Lull and Lullism in Fourteenth-Century France* (Oxford: 1971), pp. 271 ff.

[2]While most scholars give lip service to Eckhart's influence, Hildegard is rarely even mentioned. With the first English translations of Hildegard's works, her influence on Cusa and others is becoming increasingly clear. See Gabriele Uhlein, *Meditations with Hildegard of Bingen* (Santa Fe: 1983) and Matthew Fox, *Illuminations of Hildegard of Bingen* (Santa Fe: 1985).

[3]Ibid, pp. 30-33. In regard to Eckhart's relationship to nature, see Fox's introduction of *Breakthrough: Meister Eckhart's Creation Spirituality in New Translation* (New York: 1980), especially pp. 30-35. Also see pp. 75-82.

[4]Pauline M. Watt's *Nicolaus of Cusanus: A Fifteenth-Century Vision of Man* (Leiden: 1982), p. 23.

[5]It is not known exactly when the *De Coniecturis* was written. Cusa, however, makes reference to it in the second book of the *De Docta Ignorantia*, which suggests that both works were conceived around the same time.

[6]See Fox's *Breakthrough*, p. 185, and endnote no. 6 to Sermon Twelve, p. 555.

[7]*Nicholas of Cusa: Idiota de Mente—The Layman: About Mind*, Clyde L. Miller, trans. (New York: 1979), pp. 62-63.

[8]James F. Yockey, *Patriarchy and Self-Organization: Cosmic Observations on the Emergence of Earth-Mind*, thesis.

[9]*De Mente*, p. 62

[10]Nicolai De Cusa, *Opera Omnia*, Iussu et auctoritate Acadamiae Literarum Heidlebergensis ad Codicum Fidem edita, Felix Meiner (Leipzig: 1932-   ). *De Docta Ignorantia*, pp. 1-2. Hereafter citings from the critical edition shall be as follows:
>De Docta Ignorantia: DDI
>De Coniecturis: DC
>De Pace Fidei: DPF

[11]*Idiota De Mente*, pp. 43 and 63.

[12]For a discussion of panentheism, see Matthew Fox, *Original Blessing* (Santa Fe: 1984), pp. 88-92.

[13]DC, p. 18

[14]DC, pp. 7-8.

[15]DDI, 2.3, p. 70

[16]See Fox's *Breakthrough*, pp. 57-82

[17]DPF 1.3, pp. 4-5.

[18]DC, p. 8.

[19]*Idiota De Mente*, p. 65.

[20]Ibid.

[21]Ibid, p. 67.

[22]Matthew Fox, "Meister Eckhart on the Fourfold Path of a Creation-Centered Spiritual Journey" in Matthew Fox, ed., *Western Spirituality: Historical Roots, Ecumenical Routes* (Santa Fe: 1981).

[23]DC, pp. 15-17.

[24]See, for example, Erich Jantsch, *The Self-Organizing Universe*, p. 224 (New York: 1980).

[25]Hildegard must be credited for naming the real meaning of speculative theology. As Fox notes in *Illuminations*, p. 104, "Speculative knowledge does not mean for Hildegard what it has come to mean in an era of rationalism . . . namely abstract and airy speculating, or as *Webster's Dictionary* puts it, to review something idly or inconclusively. Hildegard writes, "This knowledge is speculative because it is like a mirror. . . ."

[26]For a complete study of pre-patriarchal myth, see Barbara G. Walker, *The Woman's Encyclopedia of Myths and Secrets*, (San Francisco: 1983).

MIND
THE IMAGE OF GOD/DESS

Path I: *The Via Positiva*

Just as
the absolute, Divine Mind
        is all
that is in everything
that is,

so the human mind
        is the all
        of its dreams.

*

Divinity
is the enfolding and unfolding of
everything that is.
Divinity
is in all things in such a way
       that all things are in divinity.

Mind itself
supposing itself
to encompass, survey,
and comprehend all things
thus concludes
       that it is in everything
       and everything is in it.

*

I return again to the divine
enfolding and unfolding.
Returning,
I go in
and out
      of divinity.

When I find God/dess
as the power that unfolds
      I go out.
When I find God/dess
as the power that enfolds
      I go in.
When I find God/dess
as the power that enfolds and unfolds
I go in and out simultaneously.

✳

Thus it is that the understanding
that does not taste clear,
wisdom is like an eye in the darkness.
It is an eye but it does not see
        because it is not in light.
And because it lacks a delicious life,
which consists in seeing, it is in pain and torment.
        And this is death, not life.

✳

So, too, the mind that turns to
anything other than the food of eternal wisdom
will find itself outside of life,
bound up in the chains of ignorance,
        a corpse, not a living body.
This is the final torment, to have a mind
and never to understand.

For who would not die to obtain such wisdom
from which stems all beauty, all the sweetness of life
and everything worth loving.

Wisdom is such a pleasant food
that it satisfies without diminishing the appetite
and thus provides a delight
        that never ceases.

*

The person who finds a treasure
in a field cannot rejoice if the field
is owned by another person.
It is for that reason that this same person
will sell all he or she has to purchase the field
and so gain that treasure.

Eternal wisdom will not be obtained
unless the possessor owns nothing.

The spirit of wisdom
dwells in a pure field,
in a wisdom-pure field.

*

The son of the Divine
plants himself in his field
in order to bring forth
        the children of the Divine.
Where the eternal wisdom dwells,
there is the Lord's field which
bears immortal fruit.

Wisdom cultivates the field
of the virtues
and produces the fruits
        of the spirit.
True science roots us in the Earth.

✳

In the handiwork which
is humanity
how greatly does the power
of wisdom burn forth:
          in the parts of the body
their arrangement,
the infused vitality,
the harmony and movement
          of the various organs;
and, finally,
in the spirit of the mind
which is capable of
wondrous arts.

✳

O, King/Queen
of the Universe,
it pleased you that
the body of humanity
formed from the dust of the Earth
be animated by you
     so that your unutterable power
     might burn forth.
You created along with humanity
all those things through which we,
aroused by the things which delight our senses,
are able to raise the eyes of our minds to you.

*

Divinity
has all things
which are found in creatures.

       Divine having is Being.
Therefore,
whatever is found in creatures
is found in the Divine.
       This is to say it is divine.

Humans are therefore divine,
but not absolutely
since we are human.

       ✳

We are, as it were,
        a human deity.
Humans are also the universe,
but not absolutely
since we are human.

Humanity is therefore a microcosm,
or in truth,
        a human universe.

Thus humanity itself encloses
both God and the universe
in its human power.

*

A creature is not God/dess
nor is it nothingness;
it is, in a sense, behind God/dess
and in front of nothingness.
Or rather,
creatures stand
      between God/dess
      and nothingness.

        ✳

What is attributable to God/dess
is the fact that a creature has unity, autonomy,
          and is in harmony with the universe.
However, one's unity lies amidst plurality,
one's individual autonomy amidst chaos,
          and one's harmony amidst dissonance.

Is it possible then for anyone to understand the
being of a creature by simultaneously considering
the absolute necessity which produced it and the
contingency which is
          an indispensable condition of existence?

*

Who can understand how all things,
while different from one another
because of their unique nature,
are an image of that
          one unique, infinite form?
It is as though God/dess "happens" a creature
in the same way that a woman "happens" a man.

Only in a finite fashion
          is the infinite form received.

                    ✳

Every creature is, so to speak,
a "God/dess-creature," a "finite-infinity."
Which means that no creature's existence could be
more perfect than it is.

✳

Manyness is nothing
but unity in participation.
That is why all the variations
which are found in creatures
are a participation
in the one infinite power
which fills the entire home
        of the divine creation.

How is it possible, then,
for anyone to
understand
how God/dess is the form of all being
without being involved in creation?

✳

It is as if the Creator had said,
    "Let me be created"
and because God/dess, who is
eternity itself, could not be brought
into being, that which could most
resemble the Creator
    was made.

*

Every creature, as such, is perfect
even if by comparison with others
it may seem imperfect.

None desires greater nobility than
any other; each loves that nobility
which God/dess has given it
while striving to maintain
and intensify that nobility.

＊

God/dess is neither in the sun
nor the moon, yet still in an absolute way
God/dess is in them
what they are,
so the universe is neither in the sun
nor the moon, yet still, in a relative way
it is in them
what they are.

*

It is evident that
in the universe
identity consists in diversity
just as unity consists in plurality.

The universe, then,
is not the sun nor the moon,
Yet it is
      the sun in the sun
      and the moon in the moon.
On the other hand,
God/dess is not
the sun in the sun
nor the moon in the moon
but is singularly and unitarily
      what the sun and moon are.

Universe means universality
that is, unity of distinct realities.

*

In fact,
in every creature
the universe is the creature;
consequently, each creature receives the whole,
so that in any creature all creatures
        are found, in a relative way.
The universe is in each person
in such a way that each person
        is in it
and so
every person
in the universe
        is the universe.

*

We see that the Creator
has bestowed in all creatures
the natural desire to B*e*, with the
fullest measure of B*e-ing* that is in
harmony with each creature's particular nature.
There is also in each creature
      a natural discernment
which compliments a creature's natural desire
and allows the creature to reach is destiny
in that object towards which it is allured
      by the weight of its own nature.

          *

This is the lover's most joyful comprehension
when he or she comprehends
the incomprehensible loveliness
of that which is loved.

*

Life itself
is a mindful spirit
having within itself
a certain innate enchantment
through which it searches
with great desire
          the very font of its own life.

Without that enchantment
life could neither
seek after itself
          nor know when it had found itself.

✳

50

Every spirit
finds it sweet
to gravitate continually
        to the very center of life.
For
a persistent
and continual gravitation toward life
is the elemental element
        of ever-growing happiness.

What do the living seek but life?
The existent but existence?
What does love seek
but to be loved?

*

MINDFUL IGNORANCE

Path II: *The Via Negativa*

Truly the intricacies in the created order
and the suitable adaption of human knowledge
to divine knowledge
so far exceeds the reach of human reason
that Socrates believed
he knew nothing
            except his own ignorance.

If, therefore, this is true concerning divinity,
then the difficulty which befalls us
            is like that of night owls
            attempting to gaze upon the sun.

✳ ✳

Yet,
in order that the appetite to know God/dess
not be frustrated,
we desire to know that we are ignorant.
If we are able to fully attain this,
then we will obtain
mindful ignorance.

* *

It is necessary
for one who wants to
attain understanding
to raise the intellect
    above the meaning of words
rather than to insist
upon their properties
which, in any case,
cannot be properly adapted
    to such great mindful mysteries.

Intellectual knowledge, alone and unaided,
desires and exaggerates
    the victory of words
and it is far from that
to God/dess
    who is our peace.

* *

A finite intellect, therefore,
cannot through concepts
reach the absolute truth of things.
Being by nature indivisible,
truth excludes. . . so that nothing
but truth itself can be the exact
        measure of truth.
Consequently,
our intellect,
which is not the truth,
never grasps the truth with such precision
that it could not be comprehended
with infinitely greater precision.

＊　＊

The relationship of our intellect to the truth
is like that of a polygon to a circle;
the resemblance to the circle
grows with the multiplication
        of the angles of the polygon;
but short of the polygon
actually becoming a circle,
no multiplication of its angles,
even if it were infinite,
will make the polygon
        equal the circle.

* *

It is therefore clear
that all we know of truth
is that the Absolute Truth, as it is,
    is beyond our grasp.

The more mindfully we learn
this lesson of ignorance,
the closer we draw
to truth itself.

✳   ✳

The scholars are deficient
in that they are afraid
to enter the darkness.
Reason shuns it
and is afraid to steal in.
But in avoiding the darkness
reason does not arrive
at a vision
of the invisible.

* *

In every science
certain things must be accepted
as first principles
if the subject matter
        is to be understood;
and these first axioms
rest only upon conviction.
Thus,
"unless you believe,
        you shall not understand."

The knowledge (*scientia*) of this world,
where you believe you have
surpassed all creatures,
is actually a joke
        in the sight of divinity.

* *

There can be nothing greater in existence
than the simple, absolute maximum; and since
it is greater than our powers of comprehension—
for it is infinite truth—our knowledge of it
     can never mean that we actually
     comprehend it.

All the things
that we apprehend by our senses,
intellect,
     or imagination
are so different from one another
that there can be no precise equality
between them.
The divine equality, therefore,
in which there is utterly no diversity of difference,
     is completely beyond our understanding.

*   *

For that reason, the absolute maximum
is in act most becoming,
since it is in act
          all that it can be.
Being all that it can be,
it is, for this same reason,
          as great as it can be
          and as small as it can be
The minimum and the maximum.

Divinity is the coincidence of opposites.

* *

God/dess is
unintelligible to all understanding
and immeasurable by all measure
improportionable by every proportion
and incomparable by all comparison
infigurable by all figuration
and unformable by all formation
immovable by all motion
and unimaginable by all imagination
insensible to all sensation
and intractable to all attraction
untastable in all taste
and inaudible in all hearing.

* *

Invisible in all sight
and inapprehensible in all apprehension

Unaffirmable in all affirmation
and undeniable in all negation
Indoubtable in all doubt
and inopinionable in all opinion.

And because in all speech
divinity is unexpressible,
there can be no limit
to the means of expressing it.

✳   ✳

Being incognitable
in all cognition
by which
in which
and of which
      are all things.

✳ ✳

From the foregoing it is clear
that "being" or any other word
is not the precise name of the maximum;
    it is beyond every name;
yet the name "maximum" must mean—
that Being in the highest, most indescribable way,
which is named of it more than any being.

          * *

The absolute maximum
is beyond our comprehension,
yet comprehensible;
able to be named
      while remaining unnamable.

The ignorance that is mindful
understands most clearly
that the absolute maximum
so necessarily exists
      that it is absolute necessity.

* *

I know that what I perceive with my senses
is not born out of itself.
For just as the sense of sight does not discern
anything by itself but rather owes its
discernment to a deeper power,
so, too, what is able to be sensed
does not exist from itself
but exists from a deeper power.

✳   ✳

Therefore, when in perceiving the sensible,
I realize that it is born from deeper realms.
I can only regard this dynamic from which it exists
as invisible and eternal.

The Creative Dynamism is eternal
because it cannot exist from another power.
And since the power which births the created
order is eternal, it is therefore invisible.

This is the God/dess
invisible to every creature.

✳ ✳

The universe, in all its variety,
does not exhaust the infinite and utterly
beautiful power of divinity,
as if
a simple maximum limit
could be put on divine power.

Consequently,
the universe does not fully
arrive at absolute beauty.

* *

In the end,
the mystical study
of the Divine
leads to freedom and silence
where the vision
of the invisible God/dess
is conceded to us.

✳   ✳

CREATIVITY
THE MIND OF THE STREET ARTIST

Path III: *The Via Creativa*

Divine imagination
is eternal art or wisdom.
It is creativity,
enfolding within itself
everything that can be created.

* * *

Wisdom
which is itself the measure of being
is the animating power of things.
It is, as it were,
an infinite mindful form and the form that
gives the formed existence
        to a thing.
Therefore, an infinite form is the actuality
of all formable forms and the most
precise measure of them all.

* * *

It is just as if there were an infinite circle;
it would be the true type of all figurable figures
and the equivalent of every figure.
For it could be
a triangle,
a hexagon,
a decagon, and so on.
It is the most adequate measure of all these,
even though it is itself
      a most simple figure.

           * * *

Infinite wisdom is simplicity,
embracing all forms and being at the same time
the most adequate comparison
of them all.

* * *

Narrator:
And when the philosopher
and orator came down near
the Temple of Eternity into
a small place underground,
the orator spoke to an artisan (*idiota*)
carving a spoon out of wood.

* * *

Orator:

I am embarrassed, my simple fellow,
that this philosopher finds you
engaged in these crude tasks.
He will learn nothing of value from you.

Artisan:

I am glad to be occupied with this work,
for it continually nourishes both mind and body.
I would hope this man you brought will not
make fun of me just because I am engaged in
carving spoons.

Philosopher:
Well spoken.
For we read that even Plato
sometimes painted.

Orator:
Regarding this,
maybe Plato used examples from painting
so that through them
very deep ideas would be made clearer.

Artisan:
Just so
in my own creative endeavors,
I nourish my mind through symbolic creations,
then I sell the spoons to nourish my body.
In this way
I get all that I need.

* * *

Philosopher:

It is my custom when I visit a person
famous for wisdom to be most precise about
what troubles me and to bring texts into the
discussion.

But since you are unlettered,
I do not know how to encourage you to speak
so that I may experience what insight you
possess.

Artisan:

One does not find in books
the natural food of wisdom

I tell you,
wisdom cries out in the streets
and her cry is how she dwells on high!

* * *

Orator:

From what you have said so far,
you seem to think that you yourself are wise
and yet you are nothing more than a stupid
craftsman.

Artisan:

This is perhaps the real difference
between you and me.
You proudly consider yourself wise
when actually you are not.

I, however,
realize that I am ignorant,
a mere street artist.
But because of this,
I am more earthy
and earthiness makes me
street-wise.

* * *

Orator:
How can you,
a mere street artist,
claim to have wisdom?

Artisan:
Wisdom
is shouting in the streets.
It is simply not enough
for those seeking wisdom
merely to read about it.
Wisdom must be discovered.

And once discovered
it must be learned by heart.
You will not find wisdom in your books
for it is not of your books,
but of the books
of our God/dess.

* * *

Orator:
What are these books?

Artisan:
They are those which the Divine has written with her own finger.

Orator:
Where can they be found?

Artisan:
Everywhere!

* * *

Artisan:
But first
I want you to know
that all human creatures
are reflections, as it were,
of infinite and divine creativity.

Every finite art
comes from the infinite art.
In this way the infinite art must
be the paradigm of all the arts.

* * *

Artisan:
I turn now to the art of carving spoons.
I will apply symbolic examples from this
art, so that what I say will be
better understood.

✳ ✳ ✳

Artisan:
Outside of imagination,
the spoon has no model.
For even if the sculptor or painter
takes models from the things he or she wants
to depict, I do not do so when I shape
spoons from wood.

My art aims to become natural shapes
rather than to imitate them
and in this regard
it is more like
the infinite art.

*   *   *

Artisan:
Then, what I want from my art
is to develop and make sensible the
form "spoonness"
through which
a spoon will emerge.

Even though this form cannot be
reached in its essential nature
by any of the senses,
I nevertheless
try to make it
tangible.

* * *

Artisan:

By the varied movements of the tools
I shape and hollow the raw matter,
in this case,
the wood,
until the proper proportions are
present in it; and in these
the form of being a spoon
is splendidly born.

Thus you see the simple and invisible
form of being a spoon leap forth from the
carved proportions of the wood just as
the mental form before that
had leapt into
      my imagination.

* * *

A*rtisan*:
The true and exact nature of what it is
to be a spoon can never be made perfectly
sensible, whatever the tools or artistry.

For in every spoon
nothing but the utterly
elemental form is reflected.

* * *

***Artisan*:**
The wood takes its name from the form
it assumes so that it is called a spoon
once the proper shape in which
"spoonness" appears is present.

Thus, name is joined to form.
Even so, calling it "spoon" is done
arbitrarily since another word could be used.
Yet, though it occurs arbitrarily,
the word used is not alien or totally
separate from the natural name joined
to this form.

Once the form is present,
that natural name is reflected in all
the different names used so variously
by different nations.

* * *

Artisan:

If you look upon the form of humanity you
will discover the form of the divine art.
It is so precise an example of divinity that it
appears that no other form approaches it
more closely. If you turn your attention to
the form of the universe and transform yourself into the form of the divine art, you
will be able to discover none other than the
paradigm of this universe. It is the same
with all forms either formed or formable.

✳ ✳ ✳

Artisan:

The perfect creation of the divine art
should therefore be the art itself—
the basic form of everything
formable by art.

* * *

Artisan:

The creativity or wisdom of the Divine is the most
simple form and yet it is the only necessary example
of infinite formable forms, no matter how
various they may be. This eternal wisdom
is tasted in every tastable thing; it is
a delight in everything delightful.

* * *

Artisan:

It is then wisdom which tastes us and there is nothing more delicious to comprehend.

＊　＊　＊

So, the human mind is the form of the
possible world just as the divine mind is
the form of the real world.

Possible worlds should therefore blaze
forth from our imaginations as the real
world blazes forth from the Divine
and infinite mind.!

✳ ✳ ✳

EARTH-MIND

Path IV: The Via Transformativa

Divinity knows
that the vast multitude
cannot exist
without an immense amount
     of intrinsic variety
and that almost everyone
is forced to lead a life
that is burdened with sorrows
     and full of miseries
from living in slave-like subjection
under the rulers
who lord it over them.

Therefore,
only a few people
have enough free time
to arrive at a knowledge of self—
     to freely create.

* * * *

At various times the Divine has sent
different prophets and teachers first
to this nation, then to that nation. Yet
humans have this weakness, that after a
long period of time certain customs are
eventually accepted and then defended as
immutable truths.

So it happens that nations go to war
to defend their particular beliefs
and to crush those
who believe otherwise.

* * * *

Since you alone, O God/dess are all-powerful,
come to our aid in these times. These wars
come about simply because each faction
seems to worship you in all that they
appear to adore.

No one really desires his or her manner of worship
imposed on all. To want what everyone else wants
is mere imitation.

* * * *

In all those things which humanity seeks after,
that which is really sought is the good,
and this good is
divinity itself.

* * * *

You, therefore,
who are the giver of life and being,
are that one who seems to be sought
in the different rites and are the one
called by different names.

For you are yourself an infinite power,
and you are something of these creatures
that you have created.
No one really alienates himself/herself from you
    unless he or she be ignorant of you.

* * * *

The Lord of Sky and Earth
has heard the groans of those
who have been slaughtered
and imprisoned and reduced to slavery
and who suffer because of religious wars.

And because all of these,
who either are the persecutors
or the ones persecuted, are motivated by the belief
that this alone is necessary for salvation
and pleasing to the Creator.

The Creator is moved
with compassion
towards humanity
and will try to guide all the variety of religions
to one greater unimpeachable harmony
in which all opinion is one.

* * * *

All who worship many gods presuppose a divinity.
It is this divinity they worship in all the gods
who are participants in it.

For just as there cannot be white things
without presupposing the existence of whiteness,
so without the presumption of divinity
　　　there can be no gods.

✳　✳　✳　✳

Thus,
the adoration of many gods admits divinity.
When peoples teach a multitude of gods,
they are essentially teaching one primal beauty
which encompasses and
precedes them all.

In the same way,
those who hold that there are many saints
must acknowledge that there is only one Saint of saints
    in whom all the other saints participate.

* * * *

Never has there existed a people
so ignorant which believed in a plurality of gods
and did not also admit some prime divinity, principle,
or creator
        of the universe.

Humanity will find that it is not
a diversity of creeds, but the very same creed
which is everywhere presupposed.

        *   *   *   *

There cannot but be one wisdom.
If it were possible to have many wisdoms
these would have to be from one;
for before any plurality exists
    there must first be unity.

Humans must therefore all agree
that there is but one most simple wisdom
    whose power is infinite;
and everyone, in explaining the intensity
of this beauty, must discover that it is a supreme
    and terrible beauty.

* * * *

If anyone held
that all things are in created wisdom,
and if another person held and said
that all created things are in the Logos,
would they not be saying the same thing?

Even though there seems to be a difference
in expression, yet they express the same idea,
for the Logos of creation
in whom all things were created
can be nothing other
        than divine wisdom.

* * * *

Thus it is that wisdom is eternal, for it precedes
every beginning and all created reality.

❋ ❋ ❋ ❋

The God of compassion
gives existence
to everything
in that way in which
        it can be received.
Therefore, everything which
exists does so by virtue of order.
Humanity exists by virtue of human order.
Just as unity is that which gives order.
        to plurality,

So Divine Power
when it is thought of as the Creator
is the Power of Order.

✳   ✳   ✳   ✳

How stupendous is the order
fashioned by our God/dess.
Humanity's hidden power which continuously flows
out
      by degrees
from the center of the emotive powers
through graduated organic rivulets
where the thinnest ligaments of the animated body
are simplified and enlightened;
from there it is extended into
the cell of rational power,
      the power of the soul.

＊ ＊ ＊ ＊

Afterwards it arrives, like a river surging into a boundless sea, at the supreme order itself, the power of mind where choruses of certain spirits, intelligences and indeed wisdom itself is conjectured to abide.

* * * *

When there is one mind among many,
there you find peace and strength.
Those of one mind dwell in the divine home.

We have been predestined to this wonderful
harmonious peace from the very beginning.

*   *   *   *

What is it that all effort yearns towards
with such immense longing on land
and sea amidst countless hardships
except to live in harmony
      with the blessings of peace?

Peace is the bearing
of fruit of the mind.
It is
the dwelling place
of divinity,
      the divine locus.

* * * *

Contemplation is living in peace.

* * * *

We pray that the world
which is called "cosmos"
because of the beauty
which comes from order,
  might become this order
  and its power, divinity.

If we were outside the region of fire,
this Earth encircled would appear to us
  as a dazzling star.

    *   *   *   *

SELF-REFLECTIVE MIND

Path I Revisited: *The Via Speculativa*

The person who conceives
that every image is an image of the one Creator
understands that the being of the images
        has no completeness of itself
because all its wholeness is from
that of which it is an image.
Divinity, the paradigm,
is the measure and explanation of the image.

So it is that Divinity shines forth in creatures
        as the truth of a reflected image.

*

When indeed the human mind,
the clear likeness of God,
participates as it is able
in the fertility of the
creative nature, it puts forth
from itself, as the image of
the divine form, symbolic
entities in the likeness
        of real beings.

Thus, the human mind
is the form of the symbolic world,
just as the Divine Mind
        is that of the real world.

*

Divinity is the enfolding of the universe,
and the universe is the unfolding of divinity.

The human mind
is the enfolding of its own dream world
and its own dream world is the unfolding of the
    human mind.

                ✳

How can anything
that is more similar to the mind than number
　　　　be conceived?
Is not the unity
of the threefold threefold?
Is not the equality
of the threefold threefold?
Similarly, the connection
of the threefold is threefold.
Thus, the essence of number is
　　　　the first paradigm of the mind.

For the three in one
or the one in three
contracted in plurality
is already found
　　　　in the very fabric of number.

Divinity, mind, and number
unfold in a fourfold progression
　　　　of natural flux.

＊

Accordingly, mind recognizes
in the numerical likeness elicited from itself,
that is, in its natural and proper image,
    its own unity which is being.

Therefore,
anyone who understands
that the great variety of things
is a reflected image of the one God/dess and
leaves behind the diversity in all the images,
will arrive in an incomprehensible manner
    at the incomprehensible.

＊

The image is not at rest unless it be
in the presence of that which it reflects
and from which it has its beginning, middle, and end.
This living image by its very life
stirs up and moves toward the paradigm
in which it alone can rest.
The life of the image
is unable to find rest in itself
since it is the life of the life of truth
      and not its own.

Thus it is moved toward the paradigm
as toward the truth of its being.

          ✳

If, therefore,
the paradigm be eternal, and the image have life
in which it has a foretaste of the paradigmatic,
it will be moved toward the paradigm
         with great desire.
Since this vital motion cannot find rest
except in that infinite life which is eternal wisdom,
the quest will not cease with the attainment
of the finite which never touches the infinite.

It is moved
with continuous desire to reach divinity
and the delightfulness of the allurement
         is never lessened.

*

The Divine Giver
does not give anything other than divinity. . . .
But this gift cannot be received as it is given
because the receiving of the gift occurs
      in a mediated fashion.
Therefore, the infinite
is received finitely;
the universal, singularly;
      and the absolute, relatively.
Since such a reception
falls short of the truth of the One who imparts,
it elicits a reflection or image,
so that it is not the full truth of the Giver
      but a reflection of the Giver.

*

For example, your face,
received in a mirror,
birthing from itself
a near-perfect reflection of your facial features,
is other than your face itself
      (varying as the mirror varies).

In one mirror, the face received
may be clearer because of mirror clarity;
in another, it may be received rather dimly
but in no mirror is the face ever received
      as it is.

      *

There is only one mirror without flaw:
the Divine, in whom what is received is received
      as it is.
For this mirror
is not essentially different
from any existing thing.
Rather in every existing thing
it is that which is;
it is the universal form
      of being.

*

O God/dess,
the longer I gaze upon your face,
the more acutely do you seem to turn the gaze
of your eyes upon me!

Thus, when I meditate
on how that face is truth
and the best measure of all faces,
I am expanded into a state
of immense wonder.

*

For your face
turns towards all faces that gaze upon it.
Therefore, those who look upon you
with a loving face will find your face
        looking on them with love. . . .
Those who look upon you in hate
will similarly find your face hateful.

Those who gaze at you in joy
will find your face joyfully reflected
        back at them.

※

Humanity
can only discern with human discernment.
When a person seeks a reflection of the Divine,
he or she does not look for it
beyond the human species,
because discrimination
is bound up with human nature;
thus it is unable to transcend
        human limitation.

Similarly, if a lion seeks after divinity,
it would find reflected a lion's face,
an ox would see an ox's,
and an eagle
        would see an eagle's.

*

O Divine One,
how astonishing is your face
which a young man, if he sought to imagine it,
would conceive as a youth's;
a mature man, as mature;
and an aged man, as aged.

Who can comprehend this sole pattern
the most true and equal of all faces—
both singularly and in multiplicity—

this pattern
so very truly each as if it were
each alone
            and none other?

✷

Such imagining would indeed need to go beyond
all forms of faces that could be formed.

*

And how can we imagine a face
when we must go beyond all faces,
transcending all likenesses
and all forms of all faces,
and all concepts of faces,
and all color, adornment,
        and beauty of all faces?

And, indeed,
if we attempt to behold
such a face through conceptual thought,
we become even further removed
        from that countenance.

*

O Divine One, all beauty which can be conceived
is less than the beauty of your face.

Though every face is beautiful, no face is beauty's self,
but your face, God/dess, has beauty
and this having
is being.

It is absolute beauty itself, which is the form
that gives being to every beautiful form.

*

In all faces is seen the Face of faces,
veiled in a billion riddles—yet unveiled
        it is not seen,
until, at last, above all faces
we enter into a certain secret and mystical silence
where there is no knowledge
        of a face.

*

This mist, this cloud, this darkness
into which we go, transcending knowledge,
is the path below which your face cannot be found
   except veiled;
but it is that very darkness
which reveals your face is there,
   beyond all veils.

*

APPENDIX

The following section lists the sources and page numbers used by the author in making translations for this volume. The sources are abbreviated in the key below.

DDI: *De Docta Ignorantia* (On Learned Ignorance), 1440

ADDI: *Apologia Doctae Ignorantiae* (In Defense of Learned Ignorance), 1449

DC: *De Coniecturis* (On the Conjectural Art), 1442-3

DS: *Idiota De Sapientia* (The Layman on Wisdom), 1450

DM: *Idiota De Mente* (The Layman on Mind), 1450

DVD: *De Visione Dei* (On the Vision of God), 1453

DPF: *De Pace Fidei* (On the Peace of Faiths), 1453

DP: *De Possest* (On Actualized Possibility), 1460

DPL: *De Dato Patris Luminum* (On the Gift of the Father of Lights), 1445-6

RL: *The Religious Language of Nicholas of Cusa*, James Biechler (Scholars Press; Missoula, MT: 1979)

142

Other Books in the
Meditations With
Series

Animals: A Native American Bestiary
Meister Eckhart
Dante Alighieri
Hildegard of Bingen
The Hopi
Julian of Norwich
Mechtild of Magdeburg
Native Americans: Lakota Spirituality
Teresa of Avila

Contact your local bookseller
or write:

Bear & Company
PO Drawer 2860
Santa Fe, NM 87504